Songs for Sale

Dear Nigel
With Best Wishes.
From "Albert"

Author by
Michael Halliwell

Illustrations by
Dotty Doodle

Grosvenor House
Publishing Limited

The right of Michael Halliwell to be identified as the author of this
work has been asserted in accordance with Section 78
of the Copyright, Designs and Patents Act 1988

The book cover is copyright to Michael Halliwell

This book is published by
Grosvenor House Publishing Ltd
Link House
140 The Broadway, Tolworth, Surrey, KT6 7HT.
www.grosvenorhousepublishing.co.uk

A CIP record for this book
is available from the British Library

ISBN 978-1-80381-560-2

Biography

Michael Halliwell was born in Banbury 1943. He grew up in Birmingham (Edgbaston) and was educated at Sebright, Worcestershire.

After a short Service Commission in the Royal Artillery (1962-69) he went into the theatre.

In 1970 he opened his first restaurant the 'Foresters' in Lymington to keep him occupied when 'resting' as they say.

In 1980 Michael opened the 'Old Bank House' Wine Bar, also in Lymington and in 1987 the Battersea Barge, London.

Contents

The Very Old Sea Dog

(After and with apologies to Samuel Taylor Coleridge)
(Apologies also to the Hon Sam Coleridge,
Late Grenadier Guards)

In Borneo we would go out on ten day "ambush Patrols" up in the Raya mountains. Once dug in there was little to do except "watch and wait" at night and sit in a hole all day. To "amuse and humour" the lads (Australians at that) I would recite chunks of verse from my incomplete education. One of the more popular, if that is the word, was the Ancient Mariner'

Unfortunately, I only knew the first few verses, though I had a good idea of the story. Over the weeks I made up bits and added more to scan. I think it was the rhythm that they liked as it was not dissimilar to "Eskimo Nell" a bawdy tale that I knew rather better and was indeed more popular. One of the duties of an officer is, as well as to lead his soldiers into battle and to "show 'em 'ow to die sor" as my CSM used to say, is to educate. Hence....

Part 1

He was a very old sea dog
And he seemed to have some 'beef'
With a long grey beard he looked so weird
"Hey man, don't give me grief"

"The weddings up and I'm best man
so let me get a beer
The party's on I need-a can
You can hear the row from here"

He felt a vice like bony grip
"There was this ship you see".
"Hey lay off me, sod your ship,"
His grasp dropped instantly.

He held him though with steady gaze
The best man couldn't move.
He listened like a kid amazed
The sailor found his groove.

The best man then sat on a rock
He really had to know
The old sea dog then starts his log
Wrinkling his brow.

"We left the quay in ecstasy,
And cleared the harbour wall
soon lost the church and then the hill
the lighthouse last of all.

The sun rose up a'port in time
As though from deep blue sea.
It shone all day then fell away
In starry starboard lee.

Higher, higher every day
Till straight above at noon."
The listener here wanted away.
He needed action soon.

"The bride arrived to join the gig
she was of scarlet hue.
Just in front and in a jig
The band came into view."

The best man here he lost his cool
Yet had to hear the rest
So the sailor had his say,
The matelot got best.

"Now a hurricane began
and it was pretty rough.
It picked us up and drove us south
It really got quite tough.

With sinking prow and bending mast
We coursed ahead so fast,
As if we're chased by cavalry
Headlong forward into spume
and further south to doom.

Now the mist and then the snow
And it got bloody cold
Then icebergs of Titanic size
So big I don't believe my eyes
As green as it was old.

In this cold and fearful place,
it was a ghastly scene,
of frigid sea and frozen face,
no living thing was seen.

With ice above and ice below,
ice seemed to just abound
but worst of all it seemed to call
and echo all around.

Then at last beyond the mast
an albatross was seen.
Out of the misty sea it came
and like a long lost friend had been,
was greeted so by name.

We fed it well, it ate it all
then flew around all day.
Though pack ice fell beyond the swell
our skipper found a way.

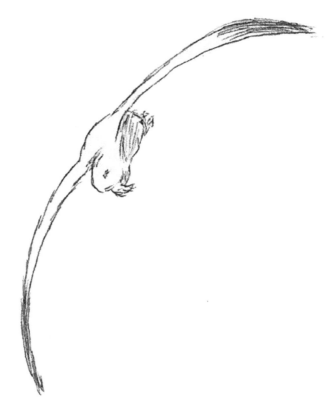

A good fresh breeze then gave us ease.
The bird would glide and fall
and daily come for food or fun
whenever he heard us call.

Come rain or shine, he'd perch on time,
for evensong he'd dwell
and though the night be fog or bright,
be seen by moonlight well."

"God's sake old man, why look so wan?
Have you seen a ghost?
You look grim". "I took aim...
Killed that I loved the most"

Part 2

The sun came now on starboard prow
Up from the deep blue sea.
Then hid in mist a'port he went
At eventide sank he.

The fine stiff breeze then drove us north
No feathered friend behind.
No bird would fly high in the sky,
We lost our only friend.
I had done an awful thing
And it would cost us dear,
For all concurred I killed the bird
That caused the wind to bear."
"You fool," they said, "now that it's dead
we've lost, the wind will veer."

No sign up high of sun or sky
Just endless foggy muck.
They all agreed we had no need
To have such rotten luck.

But still we coursed and faster north
we left a wash behind
But we were in strange water now
Not seen by all mankind.

We lost the wind, the canvas fell,
As grim a sight to see.
We only spoke to wake the bloke
From silent reverie.

Now the sun so bright above
Burnished sea and sky.
Way ahead it too was dead
And then it passed us by.

We didn't move for days on end
In that Sargasso sea.
We stood as still, as statues will,
cast in bronze were we.

Water, water everywhere,
The planks were warping tight.
Water, water everywhere
But not a drink in sight.

The sea itself was rotting, God!
You could see it stir!
Creepy, crawly, awful things
Moved on the seaweed floor.

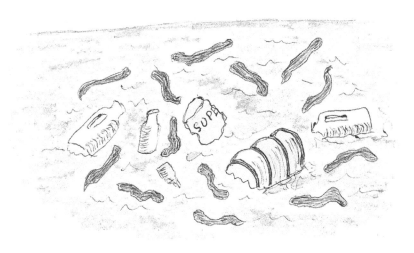

It was even worse at night,
Like the Devil's den.
Fireflies were phosphor bright
It was a terrifying sight.
A flaming hellish scene.

Some tars had fears, some worse, nightmares
But why such avarice?
Some awful evil thing beware
Had followed from the ice.

Every man through thirst was dry
None could speak at all
Dry as a parrot's cage we were
And any moment fall.

As you see they heaped on me
Such bile: such filth I got.
No crucifix" to me they fixed
The bird that I had shot.

Part 3

Time dragged on, no water too,
yes things were looking grim.
Dry throats, sore eyes, "All due to him,'
Cried one and all the crew.
Then looking east, I thought I saw
A pin prick in the blue.

At first it was a tiny thing
A speck, a little dot.
But then it moved or so it seemed
I could not make it out.

This speck, this dot, this little thing
Came closer inch by inch.
It moved around without a sound,
I gave my arm a pinch.

With bone dry mouth and sun baked face
We dare not lose that blip.
What we needed then was food,
I bit my arm to suck the blood.
"A ship" I cried "a ship!"

With throats bone dry and sun burnt face
We slowly took it in.
A gentle grin broke on each chin
As glorious sight sank in..

"Look! look!" I cried, "she's heading straight,
come to save our lives."
Without so much as breath of air
no tide to help or wind so fair
yet we will survive.

The western sea was burnished gold
The sun was nearly set
And on the far horizon sat
Our strange and ghostly saviour ship
In starkest silhouette.

The sun was crossed as though with bars
Like an old portcullis
With bright and burnished face it was
Macabre sight was this.

My God, I thought how fast she bears
(my pulse had quickened too)
is that her rig? It looks so big
but helmed she was by who?

It is her rig, but why so big ?
My God! A lady crew.
Is that an angel and of where,
Heaven or Hell: why two?

With ruby lips and wanton hips
She was a harlot true.
Her hair as silk, skin death white milk
Could strike any man right through.

The wreck arrived was now beside;
The two were playing dice.
"It's my game," said one dame
and then she whistled thrice.

With scarce a sound the ship then found
A sudden turn of speed
No sight or sound we looked around
My life blood did recede.

The stars went out, the night was dim,
The helmsman's face was grim.
From canvas dripped a steady dew
There above a moon so new
As hopes of life were slim.

One by one each of the men
Far gone to curse or swear,
Looked at me and back again,
A look of deep despair.

Two hundred times, no sound or sigh,
They dropped down one by one.
Two hundred times I heard them die
And I was left alone,

Departed souls then fled away,
To Heaven or Hell they went.
As each flew by, I heard it sigh
And twang like crossbow bent!

Part 4

"You know you frighten me old man,
I hate your bony paw!
You're skinny, scrawny, haggard man
Just like a craggy shore

I don't dig you old sea dog
And your weedy frame despise."
"Cool it friend, it's quite ok:
I did not then demise".

"Now desolate, I am alone,
me and an angry sea.
My spirit's in no state at all
accursed and damned beyond recall
with none to comfort me.

Those courageous, brave young men
Have gone to be with God.
A million worthless creatures live
Including this poor sod.

I cast about the fetid sea
then looked again on deck
bodies all about me lay
decrepit yes, (but no decay)
and me a living wreck.

I turned to God and thought to say
"forgive me for my sin"
but for my part I had no heart
no clue how to begin.

I closed my eyes, my eyeballs were
Red hot coals aflame
The ocean deep with burning heat
The leaden sky above would meet
The bodies all ablame.

What is worse than a dead man's curse?
That of a child maybe.
Much worse by far was the constant jar
As the dead men stared at me.
For a week or more I bore that sore
But death I did not see.

The silver moon rose up aloft
And never did she pause
As silently she moved across
The starry curtain draws.

The moonbeams mocked the awful scene
As frosty winter bed.
A carpet spread across the sea
In ill-begotten starboard lee
But scarlet bloody red.

Beyond the ship, as though on land
These living things abound;
They sped about, went in and out
They leapt and glowed and even flew
As silken wings had found.

Yet close at hand I could see
A sight that few behold.
Their colours green and black and blue
Colours there of every hue
With flash of burning gold.

Such blessed creatures could not tell
How beautiful they were.
I felt contentment only when
I said a prayer right there and then
My angel guard found me as well
Salvation for to share.

The moment that I found my soul
From my neck fell free
The albatross, accursed fowl,
the cause of my infernal coil
into the murky sea.

Part 5

Then nature's sweet restorative
Laid me down to rest.
I slept the sleep of angels,
Of children and the blessed.

The leathern buckets, dry as bone
That long had empty stood
I saw them filled until they spilled
I woke up in a flood.

My moistened lips and throat were chill,
My clothes were soaking wet.
Just as I had within my dream
Standing in a flowing stream
I drank... I won't forget.

I tried to move...Paralysis,
Yet I was feather light.
Perhaps I died within the dream
And am too a sprite.

Then I felt a welcome breeze
Coming from afar,
enough it was to fill the sheets
as frail as gossamer.

The sky became a giant screen.
Fireflies to and fro
Dashing dancing push and shove
As palest stars in blue above
Complete the picture show.

The breeze picked up into a gale
And moonlit was the stage
Thunderclouds then cried aloud;
Lightening too was right on cue,
It was a Godly rage.

The storm was like an elixir.
'twas like a distant dream.
Bodies then began to stir,
no sound they made, no sight they saw
She sailed herself it seemed.

Sailors worked atop the mast
As they did before the blast.
Like zombies in a trance or spell
it was the crew from hell.

My nephew stood there by my side
He went through all the motions
But did not see or speak to me
On that unearthly ocean.

"You're scary man, do you know that?"
*Calm down you silly sod..
It's not the crew that died you know
They'd not come back to life somehow,
But angels sent by God."

At sunrise all had gathered round
To sing sweet songs of praise. The sound
Flew up to heaven then back down.
First a simple single chord
as mixed on high by our Lord.
Birdsong here, a flute and harp
With nature's song both sweet and sharp.

The sun at noon was high above
And I was pinned below.
Shortly after making way,
Up and down, now faster, slow
The ship began to move.

Like a tethered bull unleashed,
She flew across the sea.
I felt a sudden rush of blood
As though a pawn yet pushed by God
And fell upon my knee.

How long asleep? I do not know,
But in my trance, I vow
Angel voices speaking low
"Was it he who caused our loss,
he who killed the albatross?
Does he know with his cross bow
He struck the awful blow?"

He loved the lovely albatross
That wraith from arctic land.
He loved the bird who loved the man
Who slew it by his hand.

A second voice, more gentle now
Spoke up in his defence.
"He's paid his price, his sacrifice
and more has yet to pay.
He'll still be seeking recompense
Until his dying day."

Part 6

Said one" How can she sail so fast
With neither wind nor crew?"
"God slices through the stormy blast
as only he can do."

The ocean servant drove the ship
As ordered by God's grace.
Th' all-seeing eye reflected high
On yon lunar face.

"He alone can show which way to go
in Tempest storm or calm.
You can see from here he loves him dear
Will lead him by the arm."

'Time to vanish, disappear
lest he find us here.
The ship will stall 'ere he recall
his sacred reverie"

As I woke we held a course
On fine and steady tack.
Still and dark and full of moon
The corpses grouped around and soon
Began to bend their back.

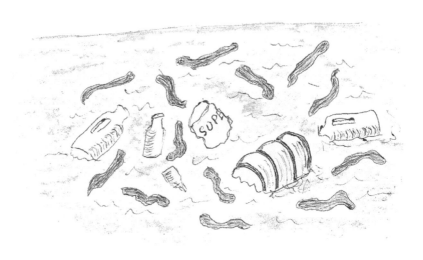

The pain which caused their early death
Was still within their eyes.
I'll see it till my dying day,
I could not turn away to pray.
I was hypnotised.
But when at last this spell was cast
I looked across the sea.
All I saw was little more.
The past was blank to me.

You know that when you walk alone
There's someone just behind?
Well I was sure for evermore
The Devil was my 'friend'.

Soon I felt a breath of air,
No sound more like a zephyr
No ripple was there on the sea
No rustle in the ether.

It blew, my hair felt cool as well.
It told me of the spring.
Like a misty early morn,
It told of life that's newly born
A fearful friendly thing.

Faster, faster, went the ship
Yet she was gentle too.
A fine fresh breeze was with me now
on me alone it blew

Now I see...it cannot be;
A mirage up ahead.
Is that the lighthouse flashing still?
My church up there upon the hill?
Will I see my bed?

We were within the harbour now.
I wept and thanked the Lord.
Is this a dream? As so it seems,
Then let me sleep amore.

The water was as crystal clear,
So still and calm the night
And flooding all the gentle pall
Of shadow cast moonlight.

The rock stood out, the church as well
That lies upon the hill.
All lit up by silver moon
As though a day in early June.
The weathervane was still.

The Quay was bright with lunar light
And parting from the crew
Were many silhouettes of red
The angel spirits of the dead
Stood waiting for their cue.

The bodies had no life at all
Yet, by God above,
An angel stood by glowing bright
On every single breast alight,
A message of his love?

This angel band all waved their hands
It was an awesome sight.
They semaphored across to shore
Silent yes but sweet the more
So tranquil was the night.
Then it was I heard the sound
Of boatswains' friendly voice
I turned my head and just ahead
I saw a boat. Rejoice!

The Cox and lad I saw them both
I was so happy then.
And in the Crew the hermit too
Who dwelt in Forest den.

An anthem then he sang aloud
(he writes 'em in the woods)
He'll save me, cleanse me, free me of
The albatross' blood.

Part 7

The wise old man lives hereabouts
Where forest falls to shore
He sings of love to God above
And talks to sailors from afar
About his life and more.

He prays at morning noon and night
He has a Holy place.
A rotted stump with mossy clump
Is his carapace.

The oarsmen came; I heard a voice.
"now this is strange," said one.
"where's the light that shone so bright,
That led us on and on?"
"Strange indeed" said Holy man,
'No sign of a single soul.
The hull's a wreck, look at the deck,
The sails are full of holes.

I never saw a thing like this
Unless of course it seem,
Like the skeletons of oak,
Ivy clad" just like a cloak,
By my little stream.

Closer still the oarsmen came
I could not move or speak
But as their boat then touched the wreck
There came an awful shriek.

Beneath the waves it echoed through
Closer and more loud it groaned.
It reached the Hull which split in two
And sank just like a stone.

Awoken by that awful noise
My body floated free.
Like bloated corpse I stayed afloat
Alive with breath in me.

A vortex sucked the vessel down.
Where it went there was no sound,
No sound at all as I recall
But faintest echo from the shore...
An echo from the shore.

I moved to speak; the rower screamed
And fell down in a faint.
The Holy man looked up to God
Said "Praised be all the saints."
The cabin boy had gone berserk
So I rowed instead.
He ranted on, his eyes a glaze
"So it's true," at me he blazed
"the devil rows," he said.

Soon I stood upon the land.
The men stepped from the boat.
"Cleanse me, save me, Holy man,"
I begged. He crossed his throat.
"Tell me," he said "and tell it true,
What sort of man are you?"

Since then I cart my wretched form
In pain and sin forlorn.
I'm forced again to tell my Yarn,
For then a moments peace I earn,
As others can I warn.

Ever since at any time
A voice within may call
And I can find no peace of mind
Until my awful life unwinds
The story says it all.

From place to place, both day and night
(I tell in many tongues my plight)
There are times I want to shout
"Hey listen you." He'll hear me out.
I have to tell it all.

A mighty roar came from the floor
For there was fun to spare,
Yet outside the blessed bride
And maids were singing there
And the distant knell of a single bell
Called me away to prayer.

Oh yes my man my spirit was
Desolate at sea.
So alone that I bemoaned
God too deserted me.

Better by far than any bar
Best by far to me
Is to walk to God with a friendly nod
At the fellow company.

To go in friendship into church
And worship him on high.
And as we kneel we all will feel
The best fix in our life.
Brothers, friends all make amends
And pray for the key of heaven.

So cheerio and have a ball
Remember, don't desist.
Who pray the best, they love the best
Be it man or beast.

The old sea dog with whizzened brow
And graying beard departs.
The listener though is puzzled now,
He's lost the urge to dance somehow
And slowly turns to go.

He left as though he had mislaid,
Forgotten, lost his key,
But he'll return a better man
From his reverie....

Ode to the Ration Pack

Time was when we would be issued with tinned rations, as soldiers had been for a hundred years. The contents hadn't changed much either. Old favourites such as Bully Beef and steak and kidney were popular as ever. Indeed sometimes we ate wartime rations. However, the Americans had developed lighter 'C' rations and we had to follow suit. Basically, it was all dehydrated stuff with a Mars bar and loo paper!

Hence...

THE ODE TO THE RATION PACK

Gone are the days of the cold Ginger pud.
Gone are the days when a soldier could
go off to war and expect to get thin
eating sausage and beans straight out of the tin.
For today the War Office has decreed
that the fighting man has the utmost need
of lighter rations when he goes to war:
for lighter rations mean he can carry more!
So from within that Ivory tower
came "ration pack, light, 24 Hour".
The joys of this I shall now describe
and you may then the aromas imbibe.

The main course would be a choice, one of three
Steak and kidney block, beef or chicken maybe.
This would be followed by either of two:
Smash that you boil or apple flakes that you stew!
There's powdered milk, powdered egg and powdered rice.
They'll powder just anything that might have been nice.
There's coffee and tea for many a brew
Paper (not writing!) and a Mars bar or two.
This ration pack weighs two pounds and a quarter,
However to cook it takes eight pints of water!
This makes it ideal for places where rain
is abundant like Brecon or Salisbury Plain!

The Pikemen

He Said that they looked an elderly lot,
"No good in a war" was his passing shot!
The radio man spoke of my friends.
He hadn't a clue so I'll make amends.
Forget for a moment the passing of time,
these men had all put their lives on the line.
Regular service, reserve and TA
is honoured respected and only the way
to earn them the right to carry a pike
to march with and guard the Lord Mayor and his like.

A sharp eye can see from deep in the crowd
the bearing and purpose; head still held proud.
But pageantry is just part of the script.
It raises the pulse and encourages conscripts.
Behind all this show there's a serious chore
done by these folk who are "Too old for War".
The TA is part of one Army alone
and they cannot fight lest some "Hold the 'phone"!
mark up the maps and brief all the stars
as to who has moved where while they've been "at the war".
So just you remember when you commentate
That they also serve who just stand and wait.
Let's hear then no more of "too old to fight".
A soldier's a Soldier till he "puts out the light".
If there's a role where he can be part
he'll give it his best with all of his heart.
Back in H.Q. the map room or 'phone
he doesn't mind and he won't be alone
and if he's to march with pride with his Queen
there's nowhere on earth he would rather have been!

(Radio 5 Comments on Lord Mayor's show 1997.
The Queen's Jubilee.)

Remembrance

They were just like me and you
Chippies, Brickies, Navvies too.
Their bad luck was they were fine
young men in fourteen; thirty-nine.

Volunteers, call-up too,
"Hello" Khaki, Navy Blue!
Instead of humping bricks or coal
Pill-box, bunker was their goal.

Average guys would then perform
superhuman feats as norm.
Physical and mental tasks
Anything their country asked.

Humour, mixed with courage won
the day against the "Hun".
"has it got my name on Bill?"
as bullets, bombs and blades would kill.

Some had paid an awful price
the ultimate in sacrifice.
I pray as I salute them all
That I as well would hear the call.

Those Far Off Days in June

(talking to veterans on the 50th anniversary of D-Day)

I've had a long and quite eventful life;
A happy home and educated well
Two lovely boys, a sweet, devoted wife
A good career, retirement, time to dwell

Yet in my life the best thing I have done
Was with some friends, once long ago in June.
I was a lad of barely twenty one
Yet old and battle hardened far too soon

We met by chance at Aldershot one day
And learnt to kill; an alien kind of life
Hunting out some Germans far away
Who just like us were caught in evil strife.

We bonded well and formed our team alone;
Cried aloud if one of us were killed,
Lost part of us whenever one went down
Then on again, his inner strength distilled.

It's clear to-day through bloody, bitter haze
Yet still it seems they were the best of days.

Crusader, Spearpoint etc., 70'S and 80'S

Cold and wet, sweaty and dank
Three smelly bodies in one small tank.
Condensation dripping on my face
Can't seem to find a single dry place.
Even if it's dry it's as cold as steel
Solid little lumps are all I can feel.
Try to turn over inside my 'sack'
There's another lump in the small of my back.
Time to get a kip before my 'stag'
Ten seconds later I'm shaken from my bag.
"fancy a brew Sir?' I look for my watch.
Hot and sticky sweet but I'd rather have a scotch.
"C.O.'s moved again can you meet him there?...
It's in tomorrow's code Sir...we haven't got a spare.
R.V.'s the wood Sir, twenty minutes time.
The Rover's gone for rations; back at half past nine."
Scramble off and cadge a lift, make it to the brief
From chief of staff who likes to pass as Deputy in Chief!
Then the Boss repeats the guff but with a certain flair
"Any questions?" all is still, who would ever dare
To imply the brief was wry, or worse, they 'lost the plot'
So out we pour, go back to war and 'kill the bloody lot'.
The reds you see are enemy they're over in the East.
There's more of them as they advance we move bloody fast.
We don't retreat but we withdraw and score a victory
By stopping all the commie brawl for a day you see.
Then back again until the time for 'Nuclear Response'
Which kills a lot of reds you see and us as well, the nonse.
So back and forth across the north of Germany we beat
Until the staff convince the 'Brass' the reds are in retreat.
They always do. The final day we always seem to win.
Until next year, we reappear and do it all again!

First Love

When I gaze at this lovely picture here
of the woman closest to my heart
I cannot help but hope the love I bear
is reciprocated, Darling on your part.
The world is full of many a pretty face
true beauty is much rarer though by far.
My hectic life is lost of all its pace
when I am thinking of my Liza Parr.
Your hair so soft, that I so oft caressed
Your eyes, are those not stars within I see?
The nose, the nape, the figure so well dressed
and lips just pursed about to say 'it's lovely".
You see my love what joy it brings, this picture fair and true
My heart is yours, my soul is yours and Darling, I love you.

Malaya 1966

First Love Lost

(A few weeks later)

I loved her more than ever I can say
yet she for someone else cast me away.
Forgive me and forget me were her words
as though some simple cliché for the birds.
Must I with bitterness my memory let cloy
against the one who gave me so much joy?
If I think at all of love grown cold
let it be of happy memories of old.
How fortunate I was to know such love,
yet how much more so he who keeps that love.
I shall not let this break my aching heart
but hope that time, great healer plays a part.
Maybe it was my own weak indecision
prevented me from knowing earthly heaven.
Yet if perchance I fall in love again
(though at this time I dread the thought that's plain
lest all this bitterness twice fill my cup)
I shall, I hope not throw my chances up.
My first true love, may happiness be yours;
and for my part? A mended heart of course.

Malaya 1966

When Two Stars Kissed

Goodnight Princess, please no distress
Although I'm gone for evermore.
Not that I love you any less
But I am from a distant shore.
Briefly we were close in love
As any in the universe
But like two distant stars above
That travel their allotted course
Then seem to touch, to kiss, to part
So we as well are preordained
To live our lives a world apart.
My heart will still your love retain.
Love is measured not in years
Nor days or weeks or by the score
Measure love in joy and tears
And memories for ever stored.
If you measure as I do
You won't forget our brief romance.
Remember love, our love was true
And don't regret we took our chance.
"Viv"
Cricket tour of Australia 1974.
Butch, boozy Brits beating 'em
At cricket and bagging their birds.
Just like they do in England!
This, for me, was the reality.

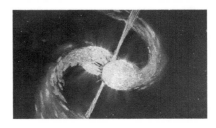

George

I had gone up to London to wet George's head.
My chum with his wife, champagne by the bed.
Then he and I went out on the town
With dinner and wine at a 'caff' of renown.
The place was quite full, not a table in sight.
'Mind if we share?" "Not at all." What a night.
The couple were married but he had just said
He was leaving; he loved his leading lady instead.
She rang the next day and told me the tale
That they had just split and could she avail
Herself of my place in the Med. But of course.
"May I come too?" God what a sauce.
So off we flew. I promised to be
The chivalrous chap. No hanky panky.
We wined and we dined. I flirted too soon.
That very first night she was locked in her room!
We talked for a week. I hoped she'd stay wed
But each night I prayed she'd come to my bed.
By the end of the week we were in love
But hubby had given the "Am Dram" the shove!
He'd come to his senses. Question, had she?
Perhaps it was just a fling then with me?
We vowed on the plane that when we got home
We'd listen to Brahms as we had done
Our last night in Malta (and our first kiss)
A week of such joy. Could love be like this?
She got her divorce. We had an affair
But it wasn't to be happy ever after I fear
Still even now when I listen to Brahms
It takes me to Malta and back in her arms.

A Sweet Memory?

You sought to escape from a horrible rat
Away for a while to reflect and to pore,
I asked to come too, to laugh and to chat
As when we had met those few days before.
For nearly a week we simply did that
With cuddles and kisses yet nothing more.
Then on the last day in late afternoon
High on the wine (and love, I am sure)
I, with a passion that seldom I've known
Bruisèd the flower till then had been pure.
Now we as well committed a sin...
That evening as if to purge us our "crime",
Eradicate all that brief "passion thing".
You asked to "make love" but just the one time.
Maybe you wanted to even the score,
Go back to your life; your husband to tell.
I like to hope you wished rather more
A sweet memory to treasure as well.

Our First Meeting

Ah yes Christina*, yes, I remember well
The moment that I met her, when and where.
The busy little bar, the noise and smoky smell
The waiter asked them both if we might share.
I was surprised that they would then allow
Two boozy chaps to crash their tête a tête.
'Twas only when she rang did, I know how
Her heart was breaking; that his mind was set
To leave her for another; stupid man.
My flirting was for her, a brief escape.
I slipped my card into her eager hand.
That brief encounter soon, would all our lives re-shape.
(I had her card as well right there beside my bed
But 'til she rang she was to me still happy and still wed).

*Christina Rossetti (I wish I could remember the first day)
(She was of course in truth more fortunate than me,
Not knowing the beginning nor end of love you, see?)

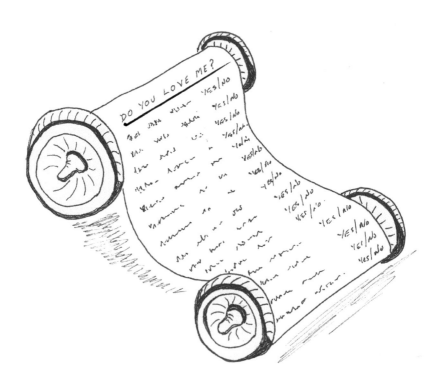

Questionnaire

Please fill in this questionnaire
It's once a year, so do take care
Simple questions, just a few;
(if multi-choice, then cross out two)
Do you love me? Careful, think
Yes or no (please write in ink)
Are you happy, sad, content?
Is your passion for me spent?
Maybe yes or maybe no
I've not been sure this year or so
A simple answer will suffice
"Love you madly" would be nice.
How often do you think of me?
Never, sometimes frequently?
Do you miss me every day?
A little, quite a lot, no way?
Do you love another man?
If yes, then throw this in the can.
Top score is just a century,
Ninety plus then marry me.
Eighty needs more work I know,
Less means that I'm losing though.
Sixty plus, it must be said
*Try harder". Thirty? Then I'm dead!
I'll mark it firmly but throughout
Will give you benefit of doubt.
If you fail me with a 'D'
Or make it clear I'm history
I'll try to learn from my mistakes
And vow there'll, be no more re-takes.

The Lost Picture

I know we've been apart for years
I drove you to too many tears.
Yet it was consolation too
To know I was still near to you.
I could see your pretty house
Any time that I would choose.
Garden, kitchen, bedroom too
Were clear in mind for me to view.
But now you're gone... not far I know
And in my mind I cannot go.
I cannot see your pretty face.
Pictures, books or fireplace.
It seems as though you're in a void.
My picture has just been destroyed.
My work of art's without a frame.
My memory is not the same.
I want to see you safe at home
So in my mind I can come
And go as often as I please
Without you knowing, hurting see?
So let me in just once maybe
That every day I can see
You again, please break the spell
(and have my picture back as well!)

Short Prayer

Two thousand years ago, my Lord,
You showed that love could beat the sword.
Give to all the world this year
Food, water, love, work free from fear.

Grace

Thank God for food, fine wine... and friends
For friendship really never ends;
It lasts beyond the grave, as love,
The greatest gift from God above.

Sin a Little

Dearest Biddy it is no crime
To sin a bit from time to time
You'll be forgiven especially
But only if you sin with me
The reason I am sure you know
You cannot help your love to show.
I am caught in such a bind
And true love is so hard to find.
What really now just breaks my heart
Is being still so far apart.
Missing you and love you too
When can I sin again with you?

Mother

I loved you 'ere I knew the word
Safe within you still unheard
I loved you in my tender years
Through childhood joy and teenage tears
I loved you when I took a wife
Still, you were Lodestar of my life
I loved you in senility
Even though you knew not me
I love you still although you're gone
My love for you will still live on
(Mike Halliwell)

January 2012

Fifty

A Rose is fairest when mature and strong
As younger buds fast fade; they have no roots
To nurture blooms, give scent all summer long
And had no time to foster stronger shoots.
Just like a rose, you too are in your prime
With lovely buds (your daughters), blooming too.
Recall that I knew you at such a time
When life was fun and all our cares were few.
Years have passed and like a blinded man
I see you now as 'fairest in the show'
The sweetest flower of all those I have scanned
And even more my ardour seems to grow.
Enjoy your birthday; may your future life
Be sweet perfumed, strong roots, a garden fair.
No bitterness or any kind of strife
Should blight that bloom for whom I truly care.
Remember on your journey, short or long
When roses need support, that I am strong.

A Dream

I dreamt I had flown away to the moon
I looked back toward our beautiful earth,
Peaceful and blue and clouded her girth.
Like a delicate, breakable, porcelain plate;
No sign from up here of the anger and hate.
It looked so at peace when viewed from afar;
No famine or fear and no sign of war.
I wished at that moment that I could be God;
Could end all the strife with simply a nod.
Anyone then who stepped out of line
Would get a quick clout; retribution divine.
I would not impose or banish all creeds
As language and habit create different needs
But would then insist that all should agree
To love one another and not just for me.
There may well be those in far distant parts
Who have taken their own Gods to their hearts.
All the great faiths in that near perfect world
Would succour each other, not reach for the sword.
They have much in common and most would agree
With those commandments you had once from me.
"Your tiny old world can hardly be seen
On the intergalactic, megamax screen.
Yet in a remarkably short space of time
You have wrecked it with rubbish, with hatred and crime.
So clean up your act, pollution as well,
Or else very soon your earth will be hell.
Remember as well although God of Love,
I'm destroyer of worlds, so now make your move.
You've done pretty well in science and art
But now is the time to learn from your heart.
Life is too precious, life's not a game
So stop all the killing. STOP IN GOD'S NAME."

Ecumenical Millennium Prayer

Oh Lord, who is above us all
Grant us this Millennium Call.
Be we Sikh, Muslim or Jew,
Christian, Buddhist or Hindu.
Give to all the World this year
food, water, love, work free from fear.
Forgive the wrongs that cloud our past
and those of generations passed.
Whether through some ethnic cause
or racial or religious wars.
Grant to all those injured thus
the grace for them to forgive us.
Let not the sins of years gone by
cast shadows on posterity.
We will not blame the child unborn
for evils of the past but mourn
the wrongs of history. Let us learn
to trust each other as our own.
Forgive the errors man has made
but let him never be afraid
to venture for a better life;
safer, healthy, free from strife.
As this special time arrives
make it really change our lives.
Let us find the time to care
for those less lucky everywhere.
Teach us to know that if just one
small act can help bring out the sun
for those less fortunate than we,
a thousand CAN change history.

9/9/99

53

Butterflies

Butterflies are best left on the wing
not captured, killed and kept inside a drawer.
Posterity might gain a lovely thing
to frame and gaze on thus for evermore.
Their life is short so let their beauty bring
enchantment as they briefly glide and soar.
'tis true of hearts, though they be won or lost
they cannot be imprisoned, locked away
but left to fly, by any storm be tossed
until they land at will, perchance to stay.
Fly free my Devon beauty; maybe you
on one such flight alight beside me too.

On the Death of My Father

My Father departed last Saturday night.
It was no surprise but still quite a fright.
When last time I left as I turned at the door,
I thought, as I thought so often before
In these recent weeks, "Will I see him again?"
"Is this my last sight of a wonderful man?"
In years to come I will see him so clear
In my mind; in my thoughts – memories dear.
Not as an incontinent, invalid frame
(yet eyes still alert and watching the game)
But striding the cliffs along with his dogs
And chiding us all as "tardy old clogs."
Or mowing the lawn and burning the weeds
Of his beautiful garden or planting the seeds.
Amusing the children just as he had done
With his own years ago, come rain or come sun.
"Tin can the bobby" – a game of his own –
Invented for us in the soft Devon dunes.
Beating us all with racquet or bat,
Then letting us win (we didn't know that).
Supporting us all through thick and through thin,
For fifty fine years with our family and kin.
A wonderful Hubby, Grandfather and Dad
And the truest of friends, his friends ever had.

Do Not Stand at my Grave and Stare

Do not stand at my grave and stare
I am not dead, I lie not there.
Think of the scented rose; it's me
Wafting gently, proudly, free.
Or the silent butterfly:
Such beauty has but weeks to die.
Perhaps the crashing angry sea
Causes you to think of me.
It matters not the when and why
God took me, left my corpse to die.
So long as when (or if?) you do
Think gentle thoughts as I, of you.
Man makes "things" and creates strife,
God alone can create life.
Whenever then you think of me
Cherish any life you see.

(Written for my father's funeral but from an idea

I had for many years from late Bdr Cummins RA killed in
Northern Ireland.

It is thought that he, likewise, borrowed the theme.)

Bergerac

How can I win your love with simple words
when actions, so they say speak far more loud?
I need some help, soft music, singing birds
To give me courage and to make you proud
Of me my love. I am no Bergerac
Who won his sweet Roxanne with words alone.
It's so much harder though to win love back
When th'ardent lover's many faults are known.
Briefly with me we soared up to the stars
Until I plunged you into deep despair.
So now I have to raise you twice as far
And words alone can never take us there.
Help me my love and tell me what to do
To win your heart and start our love anew.

"Supersonic"

"Supersonic at your will"
said radio link his girlfriend Gill.
We know of pilot, Andy's grit
and courage waiting in the pit
to be the fastest man on land.
Remember then his lovers hand
in helping him to keep his nerve
through all the years with cool reserve.
They must've talked on through the night
"It's safe, OK? I'll be alright."
Reassuring words to give
but record books are littered with
courageous names who said the same
to lovers, wives, yet 'lost the game'.
So salute the brave unheard
supporters in whose love they shared
in trust, technology and God
in realms where man had never trod.

(Thrust SST breaks world speed record).

Come Friendly Bomb

Come friendly bomb; no not on Slough,
There's another target now.
Faraday House, it's in the city,
the top two floors; it's such a pity
that old St Paul's is screened from sight
by this hideous fifties blight.
"Jerry built" to fill a crater
with no thought of view till later
(you could not take the famous shot
of burning London from that spot).
Many post war blocks as these
are coming down at last. So please,
dear Planners, have some pity
and save the view for all the city.
Make a great millennial mark;
knock it down and leave a park!

(With apologies to John Betjamyn)

Gold

Gold, gold, gold, gold;
yellow and white, hard and cold,
molten, beaten, hammered, rolled,
hell to get, yet heaven to hold,
squandered, hoarded, bought and sold,
despised by the weak, yet loved by the bold,
lasting beyond the graveyard mould,
Gold, gold, gold, gold.

(Anon)

Raymond Baxter Recommends

A Stannah Chairlift to his friends,
Yet Thora Hird has often said
That Churchill is the way to bed
But, I really want to know,
Why can't they share a bungalow?

Sunset in the New Forest

The sky was one that Turner knew
Painted black and gold and blue.
It was as though God took a brush
And staged a 'Lumiere' for us
With stokes as free as they were bold
He splashed a band of pristine gold
Along the base of earth's blue wall;
It seemed to take no time at all.
No sun was seen to spoil the show,
Just a splendid afterglow.
Narrow, arrow golden shafts
Embellished from some jet aircraft
Were mans' attempt to spoil the scene;
Graffiti drawn on Godly screen.
The clouds, more like an angels wings,
Were feather-dusted, gilded things.
Then into Forest, dark as night,
Speared a single shaft of light
Marking out a gilded sod,
As if to show the way to God.
Beyond the forest all had changed;
The stage had now been rearranged.
On darkest moor the silhouette
Of jet black trees complete the set.
Still the gold withstood the test
Sinking slowly in the west.
In the space of half an hour
We had seen the awful power
Of God, the great Creator, King
The joy that He alone can bring.
From tiny creature living free
To insignificantly me.

The Tree

They killed a tree the other day
It wasn't much, a plane they say.
The council wants a car park so
This poor tree just had to go.

Twenty years it took to grow
Twenty Chainsaw mins to go.
"We'll landscape it though when we're through,
A bush and shrubs, a bench or two."

"Hey stop," I said, "It's on the side,
The cars can park beneath its shade."
"More than me job is worth me mate,
Planners have just sealed its fate."

In some office far away,
A Planner sits around all day
With his pencil, rubber too,
Obliterates a tree for you.

"It's just a tree, oh what the hell!
I'll put another in as well."
A sheltered spot for years to come
(until another plan is done!)

Tree destroyed by Wandsworth Council, June '98

Three Things Alone Can Never be Brought Back

So said the Bard and he was quite a hack.
Time was the first most precious, flies too fast.
Each moment of each day could ever be our last;
So time is wanton, wasted whenever we're apart.
'Sped arrow', bullet, punch or any other act
Which cannot be withdrawn erased or taken back.
I can't rub out the past; God knows I wish I could
So you in me would only see the best, the very good.
'Words' alike remain long after they were said
As memories return to haunt us in our head.
They cannot be removed as on computer screen
But may be overwhelmed by happy ones and therefore never seen.
This only if compassion is allowed to rule your heart.
Forgiveness, love and charity each make up a part
Of you, which given time could expurgate the hate
And anger, pain I caused. It never is too late.

Burlington House

If you were to go to Burlington House
two chefs you would find, a man and a mouse.
One haughty and proud in oils you will see,
the other alone in the café is me..
Both men are tall and bearded souls
but only the one is well in control.
The other is really a bit of a dolt..
Lost and alone and entirely his fault.
You might recognise the one in the caff:
shambolic of dress and really quite naff.
He could look quite smart whenever he tried
with help from your choice at Dunhill...and pride.
But lately he's lost it. He blew his last chance
of happy contentment, requited romance.
For four years or more he could sample your charms
hug you and hold you so tight in his arms.
But he could not find the will just to say
"I love you and need you, let's marry today"
And so after months of half-hearted rhymes
he tried then to right all his terrible crimes.
She was a lady of pride though as well
her patience had gone and he; "Go to Hell".
Is there a moral here then for me,
a lesson to learn but belatedly?
Open your heart as soon as you can:
to bottle it up is no sign of a man.
Don't use excuses to hide a weak case.
Hold to the truth and trust in her grace.
Forgiveness and trust must go hand in hand;
when either is lost your future is damned.
But here is the most incredible thing

I saw you were wearing my diamond ring.
I was just then the most happy of men.
The richest, the proudest, content citizen.
No longer a mouse just lost in the crowd
but top of the pops and singing out loud
"I love her, she's mine. Am I lucky or what?
I thought I was poor but now know I'm not.
There's nothing on earth that I cannot do
and I'll do it and do it again just for you".
Then I awoke from a wonderful dream
and rehearsed to myself what ought to have been.
Now once again it is five in the morn,
the breaking of day of another false dawn.
I won't get to sleep or dream of you now:
it's back down to earth with a bump and somehow
I'll get through the day as best as I can
a sallow and shallow shadow of man.
So where on this earth can I go to from here
to escape from your love, my loveliness dear?
Part of the tragedy, sadly so true
you loved me so much when I hardly saw you.
Now that I love you your love has flown
away for another to cherish, to own.

I Have Your
Words Inside my Head

"Get a girl" is what you said.
You may be right, I must get out
there's lots of lovely girls about.
I fixed a date (did she fix me?)
I still had this insanity.
You were with us all the time
in my thoughts and in this rhyme.
Her hair was fair but not as yours
her figure full with fine contours.
Shapely legs and nice perfume
but still you seemed to fill the room.
I tried to be a cheerful chap,
chatty, witty (silly sap).
No good at all, it wouldn't do
all I wanted then was you.
Strange you know, there were times
I'd take you so for granted. Crimes
I cannot now believe I'd do...
Watch telly not make love to you.
Could it be my conscience pricked
to love you then, then I was licked
defeated beaten, what a fool.
I could just then have scooped the pool:
won the prize most seldom see
true love to last eternally.
I was blind, I couldn't tell
a rainbow from a rotten smell.
Maybe next date will be ok.
Put all thoughts of you away.
Who knows I may just fall in love
with thanks to you and God above.

Missing

I miss three pillows on my bed
your gentle breast to lay my head.
I miss the stolen evening tryst
before your train the parting kiss.
I miss your cosy cottage too
but most of all I miss you.

I miss the lady on the 'phone'
"I'll take a message" she intones.
I miss the cornerstone of life
a gentle, tender loving wife.
I miss the "Bax", the "blue Ship" too
but most of all I still miss you.

I miss your quaint old Morris car.
I helped you buy it; barter star!
I miss you driving miles to see
Bistro, cricket, cottage…me.
I miss the drive to see you too
but worst of all is missing you.

I Wake Each Day at Five or Four

And you know me, I can snore
till eight or nine but no, not now
I cannot sleep but think of you.
It was like a thunderbolt
a waking dream, a sudden jolt.
Sitting in the "caff' that day,
there was so much I had to say.
It was my 'Damascus trip'
scales from eyes, unsealed my lips.
It was then I knew for sure
I'd love you now for evermore.
But here's the final irony
no longer had you love for me.
You bid me not to speak or 'phone
your final word "leave me alone".
I cannot thus be seen or heard,
all I have is written word.
No doubt that this will find the bin
please read it then dispose therein.
Two things though I do recall
amid the torment of it all.
The smile and then "he loves you".
You never said you loved him too.
It is such tiny straws as these
you find me clutching in the breeze,
that buzz around my head all day
that give me hope to write this way.
If you were wed or deep in love

I'd take my aching heart and shove
off to some far distant clime
and pray for the great healer; time.
You did not say those fatal words.
Three times I tried to speak and heard
nothing more to break my heart
save "he loves you" and why not?
Perhaps you're trying not to hurt:
If so, no gentleness; be curt.
I live in hope that though not mine
your heart is not elsewhere entwined.
This is of course small comfort too
as mine's a minus score with you.
Could I really hope to seize
the moment and win the prize?
You must know first that I have changed.
"men don't change, just rearrange
their priorities. "No truly, I
now realise I've lived a lie.
I have always loved just you
but selfishly yes, yes that's true.
To suit my hours and suit my life;
never needed you as wife
'till now but now of course, you're gone.
I know now that all along
you had become a part of me:
a part of me I couldn't see.
I never took much care of self
and likewise you were on my shelf:
a lovely thing to show around
at lunches or the cricket ground.
The only thing I didn't do
was to take good care of you:
to think about your needs as well.
Stupid, selfish Halliwell.

I Don't Know Which
I Dread the Most

The telephone or morning post.
The 'phone call "leave me well alone"
the missive with my notes returned.
If you rang it would be curt
God knows I have no wish to hurt.
The letter would be typed and brief:
no comfort there for all my grief.
What on earth am I to do
to show you how I so love you?
Where I Sir Galahad of old
or even Lancelot the Bold
I could prove my love 'ere long
by slaying Dragons, righting wrong.
But the Dragon you'd have me slay
has my visage, I daresay!
Set me please some daunting task.
A challenge is all I seek to ask.
A chance to prove my love for you
and show my worth and value true.
Perhaps to write for ever more
every day how I adore
and worship you and will attend
your every whim until the end.
It may not score with Hercules
who would no doubt scoff at these
modest little tasks – but wait –
we alone control our fate.
If such brings our lives as one
it's not too bad for mortal man.

Sometimes I Wonder if This is Good For Me

I kid myself that writing is a kind of therapy
To expurgate the guilt or maybe just in part,
'cos once recall I said I would, to prove a breaking heart.
Either way I cannot stop: masochistic slob.
I really ought to get to work before I have no job.
I feel no guilt, it's early still, it's just before the dawn
Of another empty day. The most I'll do is yawn.
If, of course, I really was so selfish, pure and true,
I'd write this down and throw away and never bother you.
What on earth can it achieve? Annoy you more at best.
Pathetic prose, unlike a rose, will never pass the test
Of love. As if you care but just suppose maybe...
You woke alone, he didn't 'phone. Would you think of me?
I hope you would. You know you could, if only for a chat.
I'm always there, you know I care; please remember that.
Such silly, crazy thoughts as these really help me cope.
Call it selfish, call it sad, I like to call it hope.

No Word of Thanks, no "Well Done to You"

A week has gone by with no 'to do'.
No sad pathetic letter from me
full of remorse and much self pity.
I really do try quite hard, don't you know
to keep you away from my thoughts and to go
on with my life with never a care,
until in my mind I see you somewhere
watching the cricket or lost in the crowd,
chatting with friends and laughing aloud.
I quickly turn round but you have gone
just like the setting of sweet evening sun.
Brightest one moment and then there no more.
Was it a zephyr, a dream or a flaw
in my sight. But I know that somewhere
you are in love and happy and care
for someone who, if the Gods are but true,
will always be there to take care of you.

Hello There, It's Only Me

Thinking of you having tea.
Me, that is, with my cuppa.
No doubt I'll have you with my supper.
You see I think of you a lot
whenever there's an empty slot
in my day and there are many
when thoughts of you are two a penny.
When I get up you're on the train
with commuters, wind or rain.
Coffee time you're at your desk
efficient at the boss' behest.
After work you're in a bar
with friends around you have a 'jar'
before you dash to catch your train
back to your cosy home again.
I think about you less at night
with someone else to hold you tight?
… But now you're in my arms it seems.
(You cannot take away my dreams).

Sometimes I Wish That You Were Dead

Not really though, just in my head.
You see so long as you're around
sense and reasoned thought confound.
I think that maybe someday soon
you'll ring me up and in a swoon
confess you love me still to bits
that he was such a selfish shit.
More likely though that's just the way
you talk of me to him today.
Yet even were you – dead that is –
my love would still of course exist.
God forbid but were it true
I'd have to face a life less you.
More less than now for though apart
Life and hope's like love and heart!

A Year and a Day is to Grieve So They Say

But dated from when? That I'm not sure.
A diary can't help with a month or a day
A calendar date cannot find a cure.
Perhaps our last kiss was over a year
yet when I lost you seems like an age.
From when I knew I loved you so clear
I've scarcely had time to open the page.
It's easy with death, divorce or a birth
the date is the same, there will it lie.
Please could you tell me just when on earth
our love was over; when did it die?
It couldn't have been in August last year
the date that I fear you have in your mind,
for I had no idea I loved you my dear
as much, or as deep. Was I so blind?
Perhaps there was never a time when we both
loved and were loved as much as I wish.
I was as slow as the slowest of sloths;
patient you waited to catch this poor fish.
I suppose I could blame external affairs –
no money or time or pressure of work.
That would be cruel; we all have our cares,
family and health and most will not shirk.
I'm sorry, I'm drifting away from my theme
of finding a time a place and a date.
When did it die? Was it a dream
that only appeared so much too late?
Happy Birthday my dear, a date in my heart
I remember with love although we're apart.

The Broken Reed

Remorse, regrets are not enough
according to the Baptist creed.
A broken spirit is the stuff
of penitence. A broken reed.
I have of course been hurt before,
broken hearts as well no doubt
but never has the pain been more
than I could bear. I want to shout
"I love you, need you; take me back
Give me just one final chance".
I have no strength to counter 'tack:
my spirit's pierced on sweet love's lance.

It's Got to Go

It's no use, it's got to go.
I've left it there a year or so,
in case perhaps, you might seek
it tonight, tomorrow, Monday week.
It sits with mine as close as this
touching each, as though to kiss.
They served us well; when I held mine
I knew that soon we would entwine
in warm embrace and tender kiss;
earthly heaven, sweetest bliss.
It sits in dumb insolence now
aloof and distant, yet somehow
tells me what a fool I've been.
I'll miss it and the sights it's seen.
Even now it seems a sin
to throw your toothbrush in the bin!

Memory

Memory is the most frightening thing
At any time now it is able to bring
Back distant thoughts of times long ago
Of words that were said. Smell even can sow
In the mind and bring up on display
Events just as though it were yesterday.
It has the power to trick us as well
The good times divine, the bad ones were hell.
Unlike the computer our mind can reveal
A story so gory, embellished with zeal,
Or a rose tinted screen if it happens to be
"Golden Oldies" re-run on our in-built TV.
The Bard had it right once spoken that's it
Into the memory bank they will sit.
But where he was wrong was with arrow or sword;
It isn't the same as the once spoken word.
A physical blow can maim or may kill
But that will be that, the wound will then heal.
Words have the power to fester the mind,
Embellish or taint; re-write on re-wind.
Imagine if once in a moment of doubt
To your loved one you fool you once blurted out
"I never have loved any one in my life
I never have met the one for my wife."
Could she forget those terrible words
Or understand you yourself-doubting nerd?
So always take care. Don't open your mouth
Unless it's to say some momentous truth.
Thinking aloud is a dangerous game.
Imagine if others then did the same.
The times when we hurt are often unjust
To score a cheap point with the one whom we trust.
So silence is golden and always is best
As words may well haunt us if put to the test.

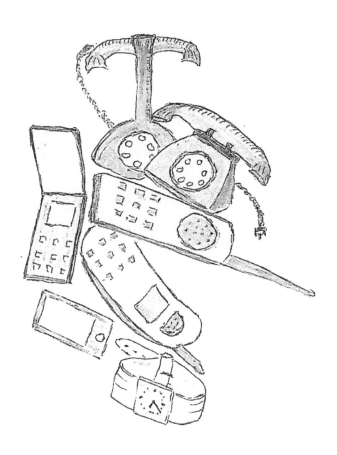

Alexander Graham Bell (Centenary)

Alexander Graham Bell
You've given us a living hell.
I'm sure that I am not alone...
I curse your blessed telephone.
Years ago it was a stalk
And tutored ladies let us talk
To friends afar and in their home.
Invasive little telephone,
Then we learnt to dial direct
And automatically connect
To anyone in any place.
(Wrong numbers too were commonplace!)
The digital exchange was born
And we could call up sex and porn,
Lonely hearts and chatlines too:
Goodbye Mayfair, Waterloo.
Now we have the Vodaphone,
Nadir of all telephones.
We have to hear others talk
Whenever we go for a walk.
It's in the car, it's in the bar,
Our clever little chatty star.
Next we'll have it on the wrist
With screen as well. Well, I desist.
So Alexander, thanks a lot,
You've given us what time forgot.
Ever-ready inane chat:
Should we give you
thanks for that?

Ted Hughes (Death)

Ted Hughes is dead: Well stone the crows.
Let them all caw, so that he knows
We all mourn his death but still have his prose
And verse to remember as well as the shows.

Tell then the Fox deep in his lair
With jet-blackened eyes and tawny brown hair
That it's safe once again to stalk and to stare
He's no longer watching from his window up there.

Who's then to tell the terrible Pike
Deep in his dark and dingy old dyke
That this grey old world has one less old Tyke
To mock and to slander him and his like.

No need to tell his lovers: all dead.
Who greeted whom and then what was said
Who suffered most and who must forgive?
Yet he has earned peace as his works will survive.

St Thomas More

St Thomas More you sit at ease
Your chain of office on your knee
Betokens that you put your God
Above your king. Yes you trod
The Martyrs path. What courage, faith
To give your life, your final breath.
Not for you the easy path
But face your Monarch's awful wrath.
Such noble trust, belief in Him,
To deny your king his fearful whim.
Did you agonise in jail
For your loved ones? Did you fail
Them out of pride or out of faith?
Would we recall your noble death?

(Statue of St Thomas More, Cheyne Walk)

Brazen Hussy

She never looks across at me
But gazes south where all can see
Her lovely form (naked too)
Brazen hussy for all to view.
She stands aloof, cold as steel
She cannot know just how I feel.
I wish I could just say "Hello"
"I was passing, how are you?"
She doesn't give the briefest glance
A smile, disdain or ere perchance
A 'come on'. No, I can't pursue.
She's so much more than bronze statue.

(The naked figure on Cheyne Walk.)

Miss X

Dear miss rampant, horny miss X.
You seem to enjoy plenty of sex.
Three in a bed, two at a time,
it's quite a sordid panty-o-mime.

Six stupid young men randy and drunk:
You egged 'em on and then had a funk.
Their faces have been all over the press
yet still we don't have your name and address.

They are acquitted as innocent too
yet still we don't get a good look at you.
If wearing a mini is 'egging 'em on'
then why is Miss X still Miss Anon.

So dear Miss X I hope you are proud
of what you have done to the Shrivenham crowd.
Instead of insisting that 'They rot in Hell'
admit it that you were stupid as well.

(Shrivenham College sex scandal.)

Dear Doctor

Dear Doctor, Nurse, Student too,
I'm a patient. "How de do."
I'm young…I'm old…a girl or boy,
Frightened, frail but still no toy.
I know you'll take good care of me
But please think of my dignity.
Tell me those I do not know
(not just a breezy bright "Hello!")
Be discreet when in a ward,
"curtains" can be overheard.
No more than three about my bed
And do not speak "above my head."
I'm a waiter, check-out girl
Or any job in life's whirl
And would take care of you, I hope.
It's little things that help us cope.
Remember please, I'm not a "case"
Just a person out of place.
I know that you will do your best
To mend my body, mind at rest.

For Catherine. June 1998

Introduction to Invalids CC

A late August day, wet windy and grey
Stragglers arrive but no chance of play.
The game was called off just before lunch.
What should we do we bedraggled bunch?
Pritch asked if John and I could play
For a team down in Sussex on that very day.
Into our cars, we roared out of town
Straight for the rural and rain-free South Downs.
We fetched up inside a fine local Inn
Where two other players were into the gin.
The two thirty start found us still in the pub.
Our Invalid team was looking for subs!
At tea we could number nine players in all
Including a youth who had not held a ball
And three of whom now we know to be "strays".
God moves as they say, in mysterious ways.
We gave 'em a game. we might even have won
And I was invited (begged even, say some)
To join in the ranks of a club of repute
Whose record is proud that none can dispute.
Since those far off days we can muster the best
And give many sides the sternest of tests.
An "Invalid" always stands out in a crowd
(the yellow and blue is rather loud).

But whether we win (yes, sometimes we lose)
We beat 'em again in the bar with the booze.
Companionship's all and with every game
We strengthen and nurture the bright friendship flame.
All this for me began as by chance
But any true player has such a romance
To foster and treasure as long as he lives
Of the game that he loves and the joy that it gives.

Dear Mrs Ashworth

Mrs Ashworth, my dear of Blackburn in Lancs
I read your star letter, for which many thanks!
I do not subscribe to your magazine
But mother does often, so I have seen
The pain and the sadness that you have known
Through no fault of yours yet you are alone.
But now I must speak for plenty of men
Whom you have condemned with your poisoned pen,
And by the way, truth but to tell
Cut your own chances of joy though as well.
I have a beard but surely can prove
It's the quickest of male 'faults' to remove
(if fault it be for no serious lover
Should judge any 'book' just by its cover)
Tattoos and holes I have of no need
(but the unread book's case still would I plead).
White socks, ah well yes, if that's a sin.
I'm guilty. It's cricket! So I'm in the bin.
to care for another's child I would wean
Is hardly the greatest labour there's been.
They are a gift from God alone
not put on earth for any person to 'own'.
Just as a death can strike out unseen
Many a barren life has there been.
Some would still say how lucky you are
To have such a child to love and to care.
A fine little chap from Heaven above
A daily reminder of your lost love.
It could be of course a slight handicap

To have the young man then sit on your lap
When courting: but surely true love would be
Unlikely put off by one such as he?
As to perceiving that all men unwed
Are weird or perverted rejects or 'dead'.
I really must argue the point with you here
As many may be both true and sincere.
Mistakes they have made or maybe have not
Bachelorhood may just be their lot.
But some single men would, I am sure,
like to insist that I underscore
"two's company" and is much better by far
Than soaking it up in a singleton bar.
The single, lone man is oftentimes thought
Unnatural, a danger, untrained or "uncaught".
Bachelor gay is all fine and dandy
A bit of a lad (and rather randy).
Christmas alone though isn't much fun
They don't put the crackers in packets of one.
Family and friends are all very kind
They make you most welcome and help you unwind
But really you feel, like playing at cards
You make up the numbers. (I leave at charades!)
So please do be gentle and cast your net wide
Your longing could yet be well satisfied!

(A reply to a letter from a young widow complaining that all
'singles' are unsuitable or weirdos.)

A Very Special Bear

It must have been about, well nearly half past three.
I had been to cricket and was going home for tea
When I felt a gentle tapping low down on my knee.
It was a little bear who said, "Please take care of me."
I picked him up and then I said, "Where you from?" and he
Said "Bearnardos", just down the road in
London North West Three."
"I used to live in Eastbearne, Sussex" by the sea
But Mummy died and left me, orphaned only three.
So now I live in "Bearnardos" – there's twenty three or four
Lovely little lonely bears. Sometimes even more!
There's only just one mum and dad, so their love they share
Which doesn't leave so very much for this very little bear.
If you could, I'd be good and brush and comb my hair
And clean my teeth and wash my face and always say my prayers.
I'm quiet as a mouse as well and don't eat much you see
Just milk and soggy biscuits and some honey with my tea."
I thought and thought and thunk again
and then I thought of you.
A lovely place, with friends to play and by the sea to boo(t)!
So herein find one teddy bear with love and kisses all.
Please be kind, take care of him. I'll see you in the Fall.

The Airmen

They too cast off the surley bonds of earth
and flew beyond mankind's imaginings.
They put their lives at very little worth
were bold as eagles with metallic wings.
Further, faster higher they would climb
to reach the stars (and land upon the moon)
Testing engines, product and design
which filtered down for all to use so soon.
Some names are legend; some unknown at all
yet all became a page of history.
They set mankind apart, for though we fail
we have God's gift of creativity.
So whether it be Science, in Symphony or Song
Thank God he gave us Courage even when we're wrong.

Jealousy

So jealousy must live off base desire
To feed its filthy habit of despair
For love of any kind could not inspire
Such evil thoughts that he would claim to care.

If trust is lost and jealousy takes root
It will, like bindweed choke true love to death
Killing all that beauty, rot the fruit
That once had blossomed, flowered, now bereft.

The paradox was clear right from the start
A jealous lover there can never be
For jealousy and love are poles apart
As heart and stone or even earth and sea.

Thus if my love I yet again must prove
It is to hope you find eternal love.

The Great Pretender

Here's to the great pretender
The king of the broken heart
Who would have guessed that his life was a mess
He's playing his greatest part

Years have gone by since they met;
Two carefree and happy young things
Had a summer of fun then both split and run
Not knowing their love could have wings

They met up again as by chance
Just a kiss and they're closer again;
As close as you can be you woman or man
With an echo of early refrains.

Three months and the journey was ended
Three months when he wasn't alone;
Yet if he had won, not moments of fun
But the best part of life he had known

Innocent

Once, twice, three times she broke his heart
Can any man withstand so much distress?
First she tells her lover they must part.
No reason given; forget please this address.
The lady then completes her volte face
(she had herself put out the ardent flame
That briefly warmed their truly sweet embrace)
"No missives mean he surely feels the same"
Third, he failed to press his earnest suit
(to spare her pain no begging pleas are found)
She scalds him thus, accusing the poor brute
"no letters mean no love". The salted wound.
What answer can I give to such a charge?
Believe me Darling, INNOCENT writ large.

Milton Keynes UK
Ingram Content Group UK Ltd.
UKHW011821190124
436313UK00006B/138

9 781803 815602